Really WILD

ELEPHANTS

Claire Robinson

First published in Great Britain by Heinemann Library
Halley Court, Jordan Hill, Oxford OX2 8EJ,
a division of Reed Educational and Professional Publishing Ltd.

OXFORD FLORENCE PRAGUE MADRID ATHENS
MELBOURNE AUCKLAND KUALA LUMPUR SINGAPORE TOKYO
IBADAN NAIROBI KAMPALA JOHANNESBURG GABORONE
PORTSMOUTH NH (USA) CHICAGO MEXICO CITY SAO PAULO

Designed by Celia Floyd
Illustrations by Alan Fraser (Pennant Illustration) and Hardlines (map p.6)
Colour reproduction by Dot Gradations
Printed in Hong Kong / China

01 00 99 98
10 9 8 7 6 5 4 3 2 1

ISBN 0 431 02861 3

British Library Cataloguing in Publication Data

Robinson, Claire
Elephants. – (Really wild)
1. Elephants – Juvenile literature
I. Title
599.6'1

This book is also available as a hardback library edition (ISBN 0 431 02860 5).
Flick the pages of this book and see what happens!

Acknowledgements
The Publishers would like to thank the following for permission to reproduce photographs:
Ardea/Joanna Van Gruisen, p.4;
Oxford Scientific Films/Martyn Colbeck, pp.5, 6, 7, 8, 9, 10, 11, 12, 13, 14, 15, 16, 17, 18, 19,
20, 21, 23;
Oxford Scientific Films/Richard Packwood, p.22.
Cover photograph: Tony Stone Images/Art Wolfe

Our thanks to Oxford Scientific Films for their help and co-operation in the preparation
of this book.

Every effort has been made to contact copyright holders of any material reproduced in this
book. Any omissions will be rectified in subsequent printings if notice is given to the Publisher.

Contents

Some words are shown in bold, **like this**.
You can find out what they mean by
looking in the glossary.

Elephant relatives

There are two kinds of elephant. African elephants have large ears and long tusks.

African elephant

Asian
elephant

Asian elephants live in forests. They have
a high forehead and small ears. Their
tusks are usually shorter, too.

What's it like to be an African elephant?

Where elephants live

Elephants need lots of space to travel and feed. African elephants live mainly on the hot, open **grasslands** of Africa. Some live in forests too.

This **herd** of elephants lives in Kenya.
They share the grasslands with **hoofed**
animals like zebra, giraffe and
wildebeest.

Elephant families

The female elephants all live together. They are sisters, or mothers and daughters. They are led by the oldest female. Together they care for the babies.

Male elephants live apart from the females. These two males have travelled far to find a **mate**. They are fighting to see who will mate with her.

Trunks and tusks

Elephants use their trunks for many things, like touching, making sounds, collecting food and bathing. The trunk is also a nose, of course.

Tusks are an elephant's two front teeth.
Here a male is using them to strip **bark**
off a tree. Bark is good food.

Keeping clean

Elephants need to keep their skin clean and free of **parasites**. Mud helps them to do this. They also spray themselves with water.

A dust bath helps too. This female uses her trunk to throw a cloud of dust over her back.

Finding food

In the wet season, fresh green grass is easy to find and the **herd** has plenty to eat.

But in the dry season, no grass grows.
The elephants have to reach into the trees
and bushes for branches and leaves.

Eating and drinking

This elephant gathers prickly branches with her trunk and stuffs them into her mouth. She has large **ridged** teeth for chewing the tough food.

Water is very important to elephants. Besides bathing in it, they need to drink about 70 litres of water every day. That's enough to fill 14 buckets!

Babies

There is a new baby in the **herd**. The newborn **calf** is only one hour old. His mother helps him gently to his feet with her trunk and front foot.

He searches for his mother's milk. He throws back his tiny trunk and drinks from the **teats** between her front legs.

Growing up

It will take about ten years for the **calf** to become an adult. Meanwhile there is plenty of time for play.

Once he is an adult, the young elephant will leave his mother's **herd** and join the adult males.

Elephant facts

- African elephants are the biggest animals on land. They can live for up to 60 years.

- Large ears stop elephants getting too hot. They flap their ears to cool the blood inside. Then the blood flows around their body, cooling it down.

- Elephant skin is very thick. It is lightly covered in hair.

- Elephants can hear very well. They can also make many sounds. They bellow and **trumpet**.

Glossary

bark   the hard outside covering of a tree

calf   baby elephant

grasslands   very large areas of grass dotted with trees

herd   a large group of animals such as elephants, zebra or cattle that live together

hoofed   a hoofed animal has hoofs on its feet, like a horse

mate   a partner to have babies with

mating   two animals making a baby together

parasites   tiny animals that live on another animal's body

ridged   not flat

teats   parts of a female's body which give milk

trumpet   make a loud sound, a bit like a trumpet

wildebeest   a hoofed animal with horns

Index